Silent Moments Of Melancholy

Silent Moments Of Melancholy

AMOL REDIJ

Alethea
PUBLISHING

First Published July 2011

Published by
Alethia Publishing
Pune, India
www.alethia.co.in

ISBN 978-81-920433-1-9

Cover Page Design
Ahead Communications, Mumbai

Printed in India by
Akshar Seva, Pune, India

To Divakar Kambli

My friend and mentor

for his constant support

and inspirational nourishment

Contents

The Mill Man's Magic

The early morning mill siren,
And my sleep used to go kaput.
A dulcet ebullient baby,
I woke up in cries, and tears.
That made my mother too,
Retire from her slumber.
Light stokes on my back,
With mellifluous bustle,
Taking me back, into silent dream,
Even so, I never slept.
In a dim faded light,
I saw my begetter, coiffure his hair,
Costumed in his uniform.
A peck telling me,
I'm off to the mill.
Yarns he spun, of infinite length,
Gossamer like,
Then woven into cloth,
That rich adorned in.
I remember though,
He never had a share,
Of that fabric,
Same shirt, each single day,

Washed every Wednesday,
With patches stitched,
To hide the rend beneath.
Nonetheless, content he was,
Smiling, absolved of all pain.
An inspiration I admired,
Lying there naked,
Covered in a piece of cloth,
My sire wove in his mill.

Colours of Life

All colours had a fight one day
They all gathered to have their say
Neatly dressed, brightened and proud
They all walked in boasting aloud

I am the love, residing in every heart
I glow so that loved ones never part
I am everywhere for love to spread
Loving and caring, I am the red

What is love without spirit and trust
I am the one that makes all honest
By ocean and skies, I am only true
Calm and sedate, I am the blue

I am the power, infusing energy
I boost up when one is gloomy
I bring hope to every known fellow
Full of optimism and help, I am yellow

Stop you all for I am the most favourite
I symbolise everything, soft and quiet
Nature and trees around, see how serene
Thank me all, for I am that green

Oh! Stop, don't shout who are you
You just made of yellow and blue
You all listen, only I stay forever
All get lost in me, black has the power

Feebly, an old white walked from side
It said nothing, sat silent with no pride
You all come from me, all I can say
Even you black, will someday turn gray

Indeed, no one cares for purity now
My ego big, all have to prove somehow
Innocence has almost lost from here
Pale it may be, but truest form of care

Abnegation

Always, forever
Smiles I'd shower
With love and care
I'd often douse her
Yet never, she
Allowed me near

Not to the moon
But up the hill
I'd steer
For those lilies
That brought
Her cheer

Sightless, I darted
Gathering those buds
As if like a last chance
For things to mend
Unknowingly, I had
Crossed the end

While I,
Sank into death
Down the valley

She ran through
Green pastures
Singing exultantly

Delusion

The silver sky, was
Slowly turning blue
And the birds with merry,
Up there, carelessly flew
I could feel around
A heaven up above
The breeze silently sighed
You are falling in love.
The river swam, like
Into her sweet sixteen
Kissing the trees around
Dying them luscious green
The flower beds smiled
And buds began to blossom
The creation, in a wink
Painted colour of autumn
Soon on my shoulders, perched
A dove, whispering softly
You are falling in love.
Cheerful I was, walking
In ecstasy, on the damp soil
Until a tiny little pebble
Pierced my skin, and
Hurt my ankle

Soon the scene turned pale
I was lost and shattered
My agony, I couldn't curtail
Back in my sanity, I searched
Around for that illusion
Sadly, things were inert
Frightened I was, tearful too
For love, I would never,
Want to believe can be true
Rivers turn into wild seas
The breeze would storm,
Skies will hurl fires in woe
Doves will take evil form

A Whimper

I wandered like a vagabond
Limitless, happy, and carefree
A stranger to the world, yet
With immense crowd inside me

Worries forever whined
Quests continued eternally
I dumped them deep in, yet
A roaring sea resides inside me

Everything I had, I wanted
To be simple, nice, easy
For riches they all left
Leaving me tired and empty

Alone here, I lay down now
Waiting for a heavenly journey
Death is just around, somewhere
Waiting to embrace me firmly

Dream

A sweet little dream, troubled me all night
Tried I a lot, but couldn't loose her sight
In a perfectly carved body, she staged a beauty
I kept smiling all night at the little fancy
A face so innocent, mellow, bright
All lit up in radiant yellow and white
Smooth silky hair, swaying across her face
And I stood there still, astound at her grace
On the ripples of water she waved her hand
And her footsteps kept fading on wet sand
I walked and ran to keep following her
But at a distance I saw her disappear
My eyes opened to a shining moonbeam
Quietly I smiled and ended my dream

Lessons From An Old Man

I saw an old man
At the metro station
Dressed in torn suit
And a dirty fur cap
In pocket had red rose
And a kitten sitting close
He played his violin
With eyes calmly locked
He wasn't disturbed
By steps tapping by
But would open eyes often
And close them with a sigh
I kept looking at him
Finally went near
He could be mad
I had a little fear
Sweet tunes relished me
I started to miss someone
It felt so romantic, and
Burdens began to lighten
Many walked by him
But I couldn't see a penny
I tapped his shoulder
He opened his eyes

And looked up at me
I am sorry sir, I said
I have no money
But here take my watch
No! He said angrily
Not a timepiece again
For it has ruined me
Despite all her love, care
Never for her
I had moments to spare
Bad time finally struck me
When my lady walked away
And ever since then
I have been helplessly
Watching at that time
But I have nothing to give
I said again
The old man held my hand
I need no money, no gift
No riches, my friend
I play this tune everyday
So that she knows
I am still there, if ever
She crosses this way
Will she ever?, I asked

For true love is rare
Yes, she will, said he
For my fingers
Haven’t deserted her tune
And they will never forget
How to care

Lost Glory

They rejoiced
Killing many, and
Leaving others lame
With guns held high in air
They shouted loud
All praise in His name
With trembling legs
And fiery eyes
I walked down the road
All worried only about self
No one really cared
About the blood that flowed
Those cries still scare
The gun shots still haunt
Unity disrupted, peace torn
Lost is the glory
Which this land
Once used to adorn
With a blank mind
Staring into the infinity
I was left stranded
Struck between the differences
Of what is unholy
And what is sacred

Paragon

You are like a rose
Your fragrance stands apart
A finely chiselled beauty
The best ever in art
Those eyes like an ocean
Calm and profound
Though not blue
Invite me to sink
Deep within you
In my deepest distress
I find you very near
The magic of your charm
Devoids me of all fear
You are a guiding force
An inspiration in my life
Teaching me to fight till end
And for success to strive
You are like a dream
One that I see so clear
You are and will always be
A darling, charming and dear

Secret Love

They met unknowingly a long time ago
Kept seeing each other through the window
Often their paths crossed and eyes met
Silence usually talked but no words yet
Scared a little, one day he did dare
Through words he bestowed his care
She smiled and nodded her head
Her lips spoke something unsaid
Roads met, both took the same way
Bonds getting stronger day after day
They were sure, they were quite close
And they rolled in highs and lows
But they felt controlled and stopped
It wont work was all they thought
Very difficult it was for him, it pained
So did she cried and all tears drained
Agreed they would be friends forever
But they were just pretending for sure
He never gave words to his emotions
Somehow so that the feeling lessens
It hasn't helped him much though
That feeling of love doesn't seem to go
Crept in bed, he missed her, and wept
Thinking of her he silently slept

She seized him in lonely dreams
Saw her face in those moon beams
He held her tight, took her near
But woke up shivering with fear
She won't like it for sure, he knew
Thought he, if she left what would I do
He never looked into her eyes again
As she would cry seeing all the pain
Troubled, he never wanted her to be
His only wish was to see her happy
His feelings, He never again revealed
He buried them inside tightly sealed
Yet sometimes he missed her badly
He felt her often and touched her softly
And sometimes in the morning at six
He sent her a colon, hyphen, and asterix
Never known, true meaning she missed
That silently he crept and sweetly kissed

Enslaved

I wanted us to be close
A different path but you chose
I wandered alone everywhere
Finding someone who would care
None could I find though
I don't fall sick anymore
I never do
For no one is ever there
To nurse or take care
Sorrow speaks to me
With words of comfort
Tears wash away
The ailing lines of pain
Pain teaches me to smile
And forget the past
Grief is not good they said
It will only grow more
Senses were ordering me
Not the other way round
They controlled me instead
Stop don't cry they scolded
At times they even consoled
Life has tortured all way through
Now I am a slave to my senses too

The Almighty Kidnapper

Everything was sailing fine
When one day, He came,
And said she's mine.
Smiled at me, took her away.
A skinny man, dying nailed,
He pinched my hollow heart,
As silently in a corner,
I ailed.

Excruciation

What if...
    I slap you one day
    And warn you
    Never to walk my way

The pain, agony, the death
Everyday you put me through
Over a baseless battle of
Me being a sinner, a man untrue

While you drank the holy water
I sipped poison, night and day,
Of your wrath, hatred, apathy
Hoping, all this will pass away

I kept fighting all alone
Trying to look brave
For a pointless union, I was
Digging into my own grave

Enough! Just end it now,
Faith, prove it not anymore,
To me, for the more you try
The more you make me sore

Then, don't blame, if
I stab you one day
With that very cross
To which you pray

Agony

Forever...
I was selfish
I had greed and pride
Fame being my only fetish
Love and you, I put aside
I have been awful in anger
At times, I even played devil
Screamed, losing my temper
My thoughts turning evil
From remains that remain
When I am tired and alone
I know how life is a bane
Now when I silently moan
Darting around empty mind
With dark silences around
Not sure what I want to find
Amidst memoirs that surround

Craving

With you not around and near
And no sound of you, I hear
I feel so very lost and lonely
As if everything has turned empty
With you not here to inspire
I have lost every wish and desire
Slowly, this loneliness kills me
And silence cuts through cruelly
Your sight so much I need
For me to be calmed and freed
A smile spreading on your face
Brightening every corner and place
Wish you could believe it's true
That I really, really miss you

Abandonment

I used to talk to you
A thousand times a day
But somehow now
I find you going away
You utter so hastily
And in few word then
Our talks, see the end
I was so used to those
Minute to minute update
Where you reached and
From where you left
Time was no boundary
When we wanted to talk
Now when I miss you
I have to look at the clock
Not that you avoid me
Neither do you ignore
It is just that I don't
Deserve a chance anymore
Don't crush me down
Like a dried dead petal
For once I had
Blossomed your aisle
Don't blow me away

Like a fading candle
I had lit up your life
Like a glazing crystal
Yes, will accept your silence
But I need some while
For the love for you
Was profound and true
Your memories that etch
Deep into my heart
Your love that I feel
In my every part
Will take some time
To finally part

Remembrance

The mirror keeps staring
My shadows always haunt
It all is worse than killing
Your memories rudely taunt

My loneliness keeps weeping
The tears that flow, I hate
Death, merrily, keeps mocking
Never in life, I felt so desolate

I know now, worth of loving
Someone as innocent as you
Never cared, I was ignoring
Finally I lost, a friend so true

I accept, wrong, I was doing
Never tried to understand
You were a disguised blessing
Now gone like a wet sand

Tired, you set away walking
Penance this is, my regret
Sure, you'll never be forgiving
But, me, please don't forget

Lost Kingdom

I see many faces, all around me
But yours, I could never see
I am trying to find you, still
One day, soon, I know, I will

I dreamt of a beautiful palace
Cherished with our kindness
An abode, with you as the queen
Promising limitless joy unseen

Together, we looked over the garden
Enjoyed the sea, swallowing the sun
You would coyly hug, coming closer
As, the night grew colder and quieter

That tender, sweet, loving kiss
Oh my darling, I still really miss
Those days so pure of divinity
Made me dream beyond infinity

But fate, one day, turned cruel
All ruined, lost was the battle
Chances with me left very few
Gone was all, and so were you

I stood up hurt, trying to fight
For his princess, like a knight
But you, my power, was far gone
In my wounds, I chose to drown

Wounds, are still trying to heal
Under the scars, pain will conceal
In dark, torn corners of my kingdom
I still hope, your love will blossom

Will search for you, all over, I can
Even if you hate me as your man
I have lost you, I know, I agree
But I still love you, I am sorry

Nostalgia

Every time I pass by the road
I still keep looking to that floor
May be a smile or a waving hand
Would show up, to this ailing soul
Troubling times kept us away
Yet, never could I forget the grace
Not missing her was impossible
I recalled her every single day
The distance kept increasing
But the love could never fade
Memories still appease me
Times she stood very close
Her eyes gazed at me
While our fingers stroked
And our hearts flowing free
The sweet times have dusked
Life has turned pale and gray
And I keep searching for her
With every passing day

Times of Change

The times are changing
But I am not complaining
For what has to happen
Is undoubtedly inevitable
I hurt you, I know
I deserve this hatred
I deserve the emptiness
I have been selfish, I know
All that while and through
And you had to leave someday
To find someone new
For you merit all the good
And I knew, One day you would
Now that you have left
I am hopeless and lonely
Yearning for our times of glory
If only I could
Have kept you more happy
We would have woven
An everlasting love story
But now dreams are lean
And even you are gone
I only wish for
A death at dawn

The Troubles & The Frights

It did frighten, it did trouble
Every moment
Every second
Every minute
Every day it did
Self consolation, I tried
To strengthen myself
Hoping it would help
But the pain had heightened
As more I kept hoping
I prayed, help me someone
Give me an end
From the angst of seclusion
What my future held
I thought and I wept
I knew I have to wait
Maybe, a little longer
To cure my troubles
I have to look for those eyes
That show some care
I have to hold those hands
That will pick me up
Out of this despair
I lingered little more

It was endless though
No hands, no eyes, as yet
Frightened again, I slept
With my woes, at the shore
Only to wake up next morning
At the heaven's door

A Scorned, Torn Paper

I was a clean white page
Torn from a dairy
With torture and rage
She had scribbled on me
Not many lines, just three
A heavy weight had fell
Straight onto my heart
And she walked away
With a fuming wrath
I tried to push the ball
Flipped my legs
Couldn't bear the pain
I prayed to the wind
To blow me away
The ball rolled
Freedom, I thought
And away I flew
From tree to tree
At times to some balcony
Happy I was, I rejoiced
But tired a little later
I lay on temple steps
The heat charred me
Feet stamped mercilessly

And some spats
Dried on me
Sometimes I stuck to a shoe
Cruelly they would remove
And throw me away torn
Tormented I was and tired
I recall those days
How clean I was once
Now messed up and dirty
Come, oh dear wind
Take me back to the diary

Do You Still Care?

My nerves will dry soon
And skin will turn pale
Shaking legs tremble more
Trying to walk towards you
The heartbeat is getting slow
Bones are crackling too
As I try to get up and go
Just to somewhere find you
Shivering hands trying to reach
At least a touch of your fingers
Closing eyes see everything faint
But still trying to see your face
All noises are fading away
Ears wait for your jingle
Your scent still lingers around
I have stopped breathing but
The nose still wants to smell you
Lips yearn for a tender touch
Every sense of me keeps running to you
And each part still craves
But you never looked back
Down there I laid helpless
Eyes closed, ears shut, hands still
Legs crossed, breath softened

Only heart kept beating at the
Doors of your heart, asking
You there? Do you still care?

Requital

What kind of revenge is this?
Or if it is not one, then
Is it a way of caring?
'We will be friends, always'
You said when parting
But then every day,
Why do you keep me waiting?
'I will look after you, forever'
Said all your promises
Then what made you disappear
Is this way of showing care?
Don't you have?
Even a moment to spare
Or a smile to share
All I ask are just few words
That would heal my pain
I hope nothing you would lose
But a plenty I would gain
Help me, I beg, please help me
Or at least tell me frankly
That I have been deserted
And that I have been ill-fated

Leave Me

I am sorry, I have said
No matter how many times
But I can't somehow
Just stop loving you
Neither can I forget you
Why do you come?
Into my dreams
So often,
When I have stopped
Even thinking about you
I remember the phone call
To my neighbour's number
And you called me somewhere far
To the extreme end of the town
Where you and me
Just sitting on the bench
Kept looking at the sea
Silence spoke so much
That our lips
Dint even move apart
The warmth was just enough
And no need of Mozart
The tunes of our joy
Sang to us

Happy were we
But things had to change
For good or bad
I don’t know
Though in corners
Of remote world
We still survive
A happy you, satisfies me
Don’t worry about me though
Your bliss is all I wanted
And that is what
Has finally set me free

Now Begins The Joy

There's blood on the wall
Do you see it?
Yes it smells fresh
As it slides down the wall
Oh I just banged my head there
A little pain still hangs over
And flows down
Like a string of relief
See that hair stuck there
Its mine, yes
Those strands embracing
My sticky red blood
Heard enough of everything
And of you of course
Tired I am
Irritated too
Will you please stop?
Or should I,
Just stop breathing?
To get away from you
You banged on
Just kept on going, on and on
To end something
I picked up the iron rod

Lying there,
Next to the chair
And hit it hard
On backside of my head
Nice it felt
I was lost for a moment
Not knowing where I'm falling
I suddenly saw a wall
Raised my hand for a support
But already I had fallen
With my head on the wall
Red flowed down in streams
On the wall
And white flowed on the cheeks
Tears! Said one eye to the other
But I did not cry
For a man never does
Blood and tears just wanting to flow
Gushed out, poured at times
Finally over, drained out fully
Lay there I, still and silent
Done was my sorrow
And there begins your joy

State Of Mind

Is it also you, or only me?
Who would always want to see?
Sailing with each other into eternity
A peaceful bliss that sets us free
Or is it just a state of mind
Into which I often unwind
Awakened suddenly only to find
I'm the only one left behind
There's no future that I see
And all my dreams begin to flee
Pushing me down in deep dark sea
As I wait for you to come and take me
In my own world, I stay confined
As to me, you keep your eyes blind
One day, I hope you'll change your mind
And place me in your heart, warm and kind

Deliquesced Memories

Day after day everyday
Even till this day, today
Sweet memories cherish me
Everything around turns dreamy
I think about those lovely times
Filled with gentle love chimes
But the care started to whither
And love seemed lost forever
I feel your breath, hear you say
Though you have walked faraway
Time decided to make us part
Very moment my heart tore apart
I search you still into the darkness
And though my hope seems aimless
I promise to wait for you on this way
Until you come and take me away

Welcome Death

Standing at a distance, she waved at me
A radiant face covered with serenity
I moved a little closer to witness the black beauty
And she coyly moved lips to smile at me
I stretched my hand to take her closer
But she moved away and kept calling me
I followed her as she kept going further
She finally embraced me, I started feeling warm
I closed my eyes and sunk deep down
And kept smiling at the beautiful death charm
I hugged her hard and surrendered myself
Until all pains, worries were buried deep
Lovingly into her arms I slowly crept
And smilingly, as always, I welcomed death

I Wonder...

I wonder if you think of me
When night is drawing near
And in the shadows of your room
The walls around you disappear

I wonder if in your quiet thoughts
Your dreams of me are anymore
When in the silent, velvet blue
The moon is tapping at your door

I wonder if the shining stars
Dangle from the clouds above
Reminds you of my whispered words
In promise of eternal love

I wonder of the lonely light
That breaks upon the early dawn
Still holds a tender memory for now
So long I have been gone

I wonder if you dream of me
When the cloudless skies are blue
Because across each day and night
My thoughts are constantly of you

Abysmal Anguish

So now finally we move away
Slowly may be, but surely so
Not by words but actions alone
You have at last asked me to go

I don't know still, if I was wrong
Yet, I must, carry a broken heart
But yes, I am confused, crushed
Cruel fate has ripped us apart

I won't ask you what and why
Neither will I, blame you ever
For it was you, your pure soul
That taught me never be bitter

Still somehow I lay wounded
Not for the end we met then
But the isolation I am left in
Gives me a much deeper pain

Love To See Me Die

You sit beside me
To see me die
And you don't even
Force yourself to cry
You think
I am being set free
You just see and smile at me
I still see all that love
In your eyes
And think
Was my love wise?
As I close my eyes
To breathe my last
And with me is buried
All present and past

My Life & Its Tyranny

I need no sympathy
No worries, I'm fine
Don't show me pity
I am not crying

I may not smile
For I haven't done it
For a long while
Ever since, I was hit

Don't ask, what's new
Nothing really is
With the days left few
For me, that, is still this

The past will be present
With no real future
My life will never ascent
For it is lost, I am sure

A barren island it will be
With no greenery or sunshine
A placed haunted by memory
Of once, dearly mine

I Still...

I still see you
All over and around
For you, my care
Will always surround

Don't tell me
I have lost all right
You are always with me
Can't lose your sight

Every time at night
When it is dark and deep
I pat you softly
To put you to sleep

I silently miss you
All during the day
I still need you
Wish I could say

You can never walk
Away from my heart
For two loving souls
Can never depart

A Catty & The Doggy

Once there was a doggy
And a cute little catty
Strange it may sound
Both shared a bond profound
They shared same piece of bread
Together had milk, kept in the shed
They played happily in the lawn
Slept cuddling each other until the dawn
Catty would start worrying
When doggy went missing
And doggy sadly frowned
If catty was not around
At times they fought, a lot
But in minutes it would sort
Catty whisked up doggy
In return doggy licked the catty
Angrily, at times, when catty saw
Doggy would pat her with his tiny paw
The two were most inseparable
Like a closely tied bundle
Until one day, a boy very cruelly
Took away poor little catty
Doggy ran to try his luck
But was hit by a roaring truck

His closing eyes kept looking at her
He knew he had lost her forever
He raised his ear somehow
To hear, her last loving meow
With a long, love filled gape
Catty cried, trying to escape
Her damp eyes, constantly prayed
Those fond memories couldn't fade
Wounds were severe, the fur turning red
Soaked in blood, doggy finally lay dead

Cursed

How would I ever curse you?
Could I ever wish you bad?
Among all old and new
You are only the best I had

I cared, I loved and adored
Only you, as the purest soul
For values you always poured
More worthy than any dole

I learnt what life should be
While walking next to you
Truth I was beginning to see
Smilingly, as older I grew

With you, life was at peace
Pain hardly glanced near
Far away were all worries
There was nothing to fear

But one day fate played foul
Colourful life was turning gray
A smile was now like a scowl
With you silently fading away

It did hurt, it pierced deep in
Yet I smiled, made tear to hide
Despite all things that have been
Your love will forever be my pride

How then can you think, o dear?
That I can curse you, think ill
You are a blessing, a cheer
Think to hate you? Never I will

Enlivening

Don't curse yourself
Don't hurt either
I don't hate you now
You did nothing wrong
For I had never believed
What I was told for long
This world is an illusion
Everything is temporary
That we rise from and
Shall return to dust
But I choose to dangle
Between love and lust
Longing for pleasures
Those were short-lived
And soon faded away
Blinded by triumphs
I reached after things
Desperate and obsessed
Only to learn
They are true only for while
Earning us a brief smile
Yet, I never liked the truth
And kept seeking pastures
That yielded luscious fruit

Frantic, careless this time too
Until I witnessed
The fact, what is true
Standing there in front of you
You came to tell me
You chose a different way
And then you had
Left me one fine day
Desolated this time
Reality crushed me down
I remembered those
Lessons of life that He
Had taught me from above
How foolish I had been
How disillusioned I was
Touring in quest for delight
Now that I stand alone
I accept the fact
That everything is interim
Nothing lasts forever
I don't detest you
Anymore hence
For you have put an end
To all my pretence
I don't feel hurt that

Our love never hatched
At least you were
A friend enough
To help me get detached
From all worldly joys
And from miseries too
I am finally able to see
Only what is true

Tell Me Why

I want to shout
Out so loud
That my voice silences
I want to blow
Away the wind
Till my lungs burst out
I want to run long
Into the thorns and rocks
Till my legs get crippled
I want to listen
To the thunders closely
Till my ears rupture
I want to sit there alone
At the temple steps and cry
Simply to ask her why
She had to leave me
When I loved her so
She had to break my heart
And leave it hollow
Everything I had was her
When her every smile was a morning
And every kiss a good night
When eyes loved only my sight
Ears rejoiced only my words

When hands would draw me close
Feet promised every walk with me
When fingers felt only my touch
Heart pumped life till eternity
Tortured, thinking alone, here I lay
Why she took everything away
Consoling me not to cry
Sure, I won't, I will try
But please tell me why
She gifted me all this today

Tired...Of Coming Back

Surprising! You called me back
It feels just like a hijack
Like a fool I come with you
As with wind, clouds flew
I was hoping for a sunrise
With torn soul and dry eyes
I follow you like mad man
Only to be left alone again
A long silence awaits rejoice
Before I can hear your voice
But wrong every time I am proved
Then to next sadness I am moved
One day you will turn to say
How are things? All Okay?
In vain though, I am wrong
For you sing only your song
Selfish! You simply don't care
Don't have a moment to spare
Every time like a divine you behave
Making me feel like your slave
If only you tried to rise above
You would understand true love
For others you have minute, an hour
Not for me, from it, I seem to be too far

For what did you call me back then?
When you just had to pretend
Am a human, not a toy
Only attended just to enjoy
My senses are real, tears are true
The heart beats too, left very few
Am tired, don't torture anymore
Or towards death, show me the door

Solitude...

Solitude, like a good old wine,
Hits me hard and slow.
I get used to it, there's no choice.
It is like living with an enemy,
With whom I fall in love.
Where can I trot, leaving my,
Ownself,
Leaving my beloved behind.
It has already taken on me.
Already growing inside me.
It has introduced me to myself,
For the first time, I think, I see.
I live with you, to whom,
I cannot lie, a friend you are,
I can never pretend to.
This living with truth changes,
Me, my world, every moment.
Forever!
It's happening with me,
They say,
With solitude, I am in love,
I am going astray

Feeling Lost

It has been long
I walked on the grass
And played with kids
In a verdant park

My memory faints
About, the last time
I played in the trees
Or just ran carefree

In the raindrops
I haven't got wet
Neither at a beach
I dropped my sweat

A sunset, I have
Long forgotten
The moon hasn't
Graced my dream

No kitten kissed me,
No dog wagged a tail,
In past many years
Oh! I simply wail

Have to live a life

They've all said
I have, I thought,
Yet there's a void

What then,
Should I seek?
Happiness, yes,
But I need peace

With the shoes
Laced in my hands
I walked along
The lush green grass

All In His Name

A pleasing beauty, crying,
Ridden by some violent craze
Sat at the steps of a temple
With a disillusioned gaze

She wept, whined, sighed
At times, looked up above
Or just on either sides, looking
Like a long lost dove

Glared at Him, questioned
"Who and what you are,
Why in your name then,
There's always a war?"

I have no rigid faith
That I wish to share
I have just one belief
That is to love and care

I have prayed to the cross
I have respected the Allah
A lot many times, I have even
Bathed in the sacred Ganga

I preached fairness and

To let peace prevail
Yet, one day, your men
Razed me, left me in this ail

They slaughtered my baby
Dismantled my entire clan
Only because I objected to
Teaching of a holy man

It is not only me
I see blood everywhere
All trying to be supreme
That's my religion, beware!

There are killings, and
Torture in your name
Then exploitation and hatred
Followed by rotten blame game

"Where were you then?"
I wish to ask again
O! You the merciful
"Why all this pain?"

Soul Scuffle

Despite desultory scuffle,
Triumphs our amity.
Like a sempiternal truth,
Afar a human bondage,
Conflate our souls, minds.
Is it indeed is a providence?
To have such an ally,
A cynosure,
Whom I fondly call,
A friend!

Ephemeron

Anon, apace,
A felicity ensued.
Renovating my solitude,
Into a halcyon!
Like a panacea,
Like a harbinger,
There stood my crony.
My misery, then,
Was just ephemeral,
As I gamboled with her.

Splitsville

It is hard to forget the times
When we knew each other
Those days of sitting at the sea
Watching the sinking sun
Taking you by my side
For a walk on the moonlit lawn
When holding your hand
Was a deed undone
The days when fighting
Over petty things was fun
You and I would always
Be the most of us
Some silent whispers
And times of fuss
Lost completely was I
In that soulful bliss
I longed for day that
Would bring us together
The passion in your eyes
Did show a burning desire
And in my heart
Did lit a fire
For we were quite sure
That we would share

These moments forever
We were so near
Who would stop us?
Then tell me so why?
Did we have to bid?
Each other goodbye

Still Alive

I am not dead yet
I am trying still
Struggling,
Since past few years

Played into hands of fate
And broken down by faith
Faith, which I thought
Taught love, compassion
But disguised it was
A form of desolation

Love had seized
The knots withered,
Feelings tormented,
Solitude strengthened
Everything was ceasing
Soon it will be over

Forever

No where you will find me
Not in remains of soil
Not even in the dust in air
And never in your memories

No matter how much you race
Distance would be infinite
Your eyes can't follow me
And your memory can't trace

Cognizance

I was walking along
The little grass shrubs
Through the clouds
Over the oceans
Under the hills

I was walking alone
Running away from
Something unknown
Fear? No. Hatred?
May be cruel isolation

I swam with the wind
I held that thunder
I cut through the rain
Chiselled into the rocks
To see does it pain?

I gazed at those rays
I scoffed up the heat
Sipped the sun
Erased the sky
Punched the mountain

I was now running alone

Angered, tormented
Yet, she still followed me
No devil, no any witch
It was her cruel memory

Memories

Each existence is a strife
Every battle a test
Every downfall a lesson
I am shattered, yes I know
A heap of crushed figures
And anguished memories
Yet, by someone's blessing
I will ascend at times
Trekking helplessly
I may often trip
Yet, I will rise again

Schism

Distances increased
With no where to go
I find myself alone
Going into thoughts
And so lonely I am left
I wonder what it is
The distance or the love
Distances make hearts fonder
I had always thought
But nothing seems to be true
No matter how much I rewind
There is nothing for us to bind
Is it true what you always said
Out of sight is out of mind
Whatever it is, you always win
And I am happy with it
As you bring me a smile
May be not long but just for a while

You – Turn

I waved a good bye
Not knowing why
Confused I was may be
Wanting to be set free
Be far away from troubles
And skip all those quarrels
I walked alone for a while
Like a nomad into exile
Still no leisure enticed me
Or could attract any beauty
Loneliness cut me with pain
And I could no more sustain
I walked back into dark
Somewhere to find that spark
With a faith that I will find you
The only one among the few
Months passed, now years too
I still lie helpless without you
Surrendered to death I have now
Hoping on my grave you will bow
Someday that you will return
And that you will take u-turn
You never came when I was near
But at least you did when I slept forever

True Friend

I died a death yet I am alive
To regain my love, I will strive
I hear the cries from the pillow
And it joins my tears in sorrow
No flowers for love to adorn
Not even one with a thorn
Longing for moments of delight
Despite all rifts and fight
Closing my eyes I still stand
But can't yet hold her hand
Afraid, I was, turning cold
Wanting to take her and hold
I accepted and agreed her say
Knelt down, made it a life's way
Can never get anymore closer
And whisper 'love you' in her ear
No gold to offer, or riches to give
Only a wish I have, while I live
To see you happy and smiling
While with time I keep ageing
I will always remain a true friend
And my best wishes I will always send

You There?

I waited for you today
But you didn't show
I needed you today
So where did you go?
I heard your call
Said you'd be there
Though I haven't seen you
Are you still there?
I cried out with no reply
And I can't feel you by my side
So I'll hold tight to what I know
You're here and I'm never alone
Though I cannot see you
And I can't explain why
Such a deep reassurance
You've placed in my life
We cannot separate
'Cause you're part of me
And though you're invisible
I'll trust the unseen

Confused, Disillusioned

Sitting in the bus
Looking through the window
As I close my eyes
I see the shade of your smiling face
When you walk-in through the door
Like I've never seen before
Standing in the rain
Nearly washed the day away
Then I think of you
I know the sight of your smiling face
And it's always here with me
Well I wonder could it be
I still know, I'm never going to find you
But I do believe
That you're standing right behind
Will I ever get? An answer to my question
Life will go on
Lying on my bed
Staring at the ceiling
Then I close my eyes again
The only thing that's clear to me
Is your smiling face
Maybe I should wake again
Maybe I should let it end

Alone I stand

I don't understand and don't know why
How I did something that made you cry
A lot I tried to keep you happy; make u smile
But I failed and we are distanced by a mile
Two little lines spoiled everything we had
Things are now rough, making you sad
I begged and accepted, I was wrong
To make you smile I sang every song
Yet of no use, such was my crime
It's going to prick and pain me lifetime
My eyes wept while I was laughing
In all my attempts to see you smiling
You hardly looked at me or said a word
With your silence my heart lies injured
You gave me so much care and comfort
Now all that gone, alone I stand, feeling hurt

One Loyal Friend

I walked across the road
From one side to other
I felt as if I am set free
With nothing on mind to bother
A happy man in me celebrated
Swaying across the road, singing aloud
Everything around too, was dancing
To the tunes of happy mood and songs
The buildings, cars, trees, sky, birds
Were playing merry-go-round
Dancing few steps in a circle
And then turning back around
The ambience was perfect too
Cool breeze conditioned the streets
And the stars above formed the lamps
Thick night smiled and served me more
On the busy road it felt like sea shore
I had finished one and opened the second
Taking few steps ahead, I wobbled
Head banged on a lamppost, I tumbled
Holding the lamp post I sat down
Looking at rolling bottle, I began to frown
My only comfort dripped down on the road
I tried to get up but legs dragged me down

Checked my pockets but found them empty
Resting to the lamppost I breathed softly
My eyes were closing, tired I was
Having lost everything shyly I wept
Into the cold night I crept and slept
A peaceful sleep I had, woke up dawn
A dog was licking my feet, I was happy,
I found a loyal friend

Outcast

No life without you
In this world, With friends so few
At a distance, amidst the dew
I still keep finding you
I lost the thing I cared
Fond memories simply stared
Now they stand complete strangers
Walking their way finding answers
It started with a prank, a joke
And it got bitter as they spoke
Explanations, arguments, tears continued
Words fired, and rudely they abused
Misunderstandings led all the way through
No soft words, consolation came to rescue
I loved her dearly, was true to her
Love me always was my only prayer
Bound by string of love we were
That's now untied, broken forever
Away and away, I walk alone now
Thinking about why and how
You are happy somewhere, I am sure
I still read her mind, listen to her
Sufferings and pain finally ended
Only after silently I laid dead.

Set Me Free

Into the silence, I slowly crept
In lonely days searching for solace
Endlessly till today I have wept
Showing a false smile on this face
Waiting for a day to be with you
When togetherness won't be a lie
Tears dried and smiles will be true
With love sparkling in the eye
A long path of dreams I saw ahead
To be walked with you in hand
Where all worries we had shred
And by you I promised to stand
Yet very lonely and alone I am
Waiting here, where you left me
Still in a hope to see your charm
And hold my hand to set me free

Squealing Memories

For years now, of staying alone
In this desolate place called home
Once, a palace like, it was
Now just a wrecked abode,
Made of hay, and planks of wood
Patched to make walls and roof
No curtains, no lanterns
Morning sun gave light
During the night, candles lit
This dwelling, dark to bright
Thunders, often shudder this house
Rains dread to make it float
Toilet stinking, broken basin
Doors, windows, floor all shriek
Just a little space to spare
Occupied with a bed and a chair

No visitor ever knocked the door
Winds thumped their presence,
Once in a while.
Lonely soul worked in the garden
Symptomising life
Ailing body had herbs,
Soup and stale bread to comfort

Bargained from neighbours
For cleaning their dirt
Often, cleaning paintings
With sore, blinking eyes
Stared at notes and albums
Painfully then,
Nibbling bread
With soup left unfinished
He would sink into his bed

On a stormy, thunderous night
The door knocked thrice
There were bangs
With loud bellows of fright
The door opened to a face
Young, charming, and radiant
"Please give me shelter,
I beg to you, O Sir!"
Quaking hands gestured
A welcome
To that beautiful young lady.
Looking around the house
Frowning, she stood
Accepting
Offered food, notwithstanding
She had soup, didn't eat bread

Standing near a painting
She stared at both
"Yes, that's me when I was young,
And that coal blackened face
Is my wife, who betrayed, and left,
Abandoning our
Song of life unsung"
Growing a little restless
She sat in discomfort
While in distress, she squealed
I stood in the corner
Staring at her
Drifting into fantasies
Of neurotic love;
Many years later

Induration

In my silences,
When moments stifle,
When emptiness echoes,
I often brood.
Trying to dissemble,
The loneliness,
And the imbroglio,
But I retire soon.
I, then lay inure,
Alone!

Quarantined

I hate this, I don't know what
The loneliness or the thought
All troubling me
Go away, leave me
I am tired, allow me rest
Toss that love, lob away detest

Troubled I am already now
Begging to you all, I bow
Keep me deserted, I will smile
Until the death, all the while
O you memories! No, don't kill
Mercilessly I pray, see I kneel

I close my eyes, you still linger
Is that a tranquil or any anger?
I burnt all pictures, every art
Yet you remain in every part
Your craze went out of window
Your voices still at times echo

You left. I know you're not there
You never had mercy to spare
Still something tries to find you
In everything, old and new

I searched around, every corner
So that every bit I could garner

Don't trouble, please go, I say
Far somewhere, miles away
A plea, you don't listen and laugh
Cruelly you are cutting me into half
The laughter, those cries, I still can hear
They frighten me, I shatter with fear

From you, I need infinite distance
I don't want to live in this pretence
Even now, I am finding every form
From where does this pain come from?
When nothing around, of you, exists
Why does your memory still persist?

I asked the reason, to my every part
Mind silently said, ask your heart
Ah, a joke? Do you have to tease?
Yet, I asked the heart, tell me please
Yes, it said, without her you're living
But without her, I would stop beating

Thing I Did...

What I have done all my life?
I keep thinking this all day
What have I got after all?
Having strived for years
Nothing! the answer echoes
For only thing I truly did
Was to love you, I did it religiously
But now that is lost too
So much I had given
Lost in your world
But you only walked over me
Every moment and always
Forgetting things we shared
And the times we spent
First time it pained
Now it doesn't matter anyway
For I lie bloodstained
Tears too have drained
The life is now lifeless
It is coming to an end
Soon I will be gone
Come and see my death
Try to shed little tears
At least maybe pretend

Somewhere, Someday

I dream of the times
When I held her in my arms
And the whole world stood still
I long for those days now
To just look into her eyes
With tears filled in mine
Life feels so empty
Without her at times
The loneliness severely aches
And I keep wondering why
Of everyone in this world
You chose to break my heart
I held on too tight
I loved her too much
I let myself fall too soon
But I'm glad she is free
I know she is right
Yet my heart beats a tune
That is sad and mellow
She has moved on now
And of me rarely thinks
It doesn't matter to her anyways
I know I will never
Find her love back

But still in a hopeless pain
I sit there by her grave
Waiting to find her love
Somehow and somewhere
Today, tomorrow, someday

Confined

Now that I want
To leave everything behind
I just keep hope
That someday I turn blind

Swear, I try always
To vacate my heart, mind
But sweet memories
Don't just seem to unwind

You cared as ever
Your love always shined
I never bothered
Behaved cruel and unkind

Everything lost then
Nothing to help us bind
One bitter day
'Bye', you softly whined

I looked around
You, nowhere could I find
Lonely in thoughts
I find myself confined

Death, I Choose

I shout, I laugh, and I cry
Not seeming to know how or why
And sometimes I often fly
Just as high to touch the sky
Yet in abundance of all this joy
I am still very alone and coy
Playing in hands like a toy
Angered, I will just destroy
All and every love's envoy
Its time to go and say goodbye
To world where love's an easy buy
For no more I can defy
And for all that they deny
Love, trust has left me dry
Only on self I would rely
And peacefully I chose to die

Quest

I haven't looked at your face
I don't know your name
In some unseen distant place
I know you will remain
Forever from me kept apart
Across both space and time
Someday these words you will see
By chance that you will find
Within this old worn out book
The fact so plain and true
That all my life in pain I looked
Around only for you, and in vain
I have only searched for you

The Final Prayer

It was half past four
Blood flowed, dropping on the floor
The wrist is slit and cut open
While the heart was all broken
He sees everything turning red
Lying there calmly in the bed
Eyes were getting damp
As slowly dimmed the lamp
All feelings dead, emotions drained
Smiled he, though it pained
It felt peaceful when lonely
With no one around and life empty
Free he was to leave forever
No one to cry for, none to bother
At him, her face kept smiling
He loved that sight, lying there dying
A last smile he gave to her
And tried to speak but couldn't utter
Breaths over, heart beats shortened
His grips with bed had now tightened
Death was near, pulling him close
It was too late and he couldn't oppose
He needed her hug, a touch may be
With arms spread, cried his draining body

Red had turned her picture curled in his palm
Her face in his eyes made him stay calm
Flashing rapidly all memories of the past
With eyes wide open, he breathed his last

Acknowledgments

"How many things are there which I do not want"

- Socrates

None!

At least in this case, where I am thankful to all the people who made this book possible, all of whom have mobbed my mind now.

My greatest gratitude was expressed on "Dedication" page, nothing would have been possible without him. He has edited, structured, titled, appraised, critiqued, inspired, publicised most of my poems.

For her faith in me and my aspirations, this book

may not have made it to the press without her abetment. I shall remain always highly indebted to you, Sonal (Tai).

My wonderful parents and lovely sisters, Arpita and Sarika, for always being there for me and giving sincere feedback about my work.

Sumit & Pragyan, my extended family in Pune, they gave me a new hope to live and nurtured my creative passion.

Jaya, my best friend and strongest brace, who has been a great connoisseur of my poems and my writings. Her constant encouragement has been a great reliever.

My friends, Preeti, Vinny, Hanumant, Bishnu for their constant abetment and encouraging moments.

To all my readers, and non readers.

Thank you, Indeed!